200

Ways to Seduce

Your Husband

How to Boost Your Marriage Libido and

Actually Enjoy Sex: A Couple's Intimacy

Guide

By

Claire Robin

Table of Contents

Introduction 4

The First Stages of Seducing Your Husband   14

Creating the Atmosphere for Strong Sexual Relationship..27

Getting Him in the Mood for Sex (Make Him Last Longer) 36

Fun Ways to Seduce Your Husband......41

Subtle Ways to Seduce Your Husband and Make Him Desire You 46

Things Men Want Women to Do In Bed59

Fun Dirty Questions To Text Your Husband   77

Sex Questions to Know What Your Husband Likes in Bed..83

Foreplay Tips That Can Drive Your Man Insane 94

Ways You Can Immediately Spice Up Your Sex Life

....114

Ways to Attract Your Husband Sexually Without

Even Trying 122

Phrases That Turn Guys On 135

Ways to Guarantee You Will Have Sex Tonight

....145

Other Books by the Same Author.......150

Introduction

Attraction is not only important in starting a relationship but an important aspect of keeping a committed relationship alive. Both physical and mental attraction makes the marriage atmosphere interesting and conducive for both partners. Your physical and mental charm must be maintained and improved with time as you get to know your partner well and as you adapt to the marriage atmosphere. The length of your committed relationship should only define how deep you can dig into all the elements necessary to increase your intimacy. The concept of seduction demands that the longer your marriage, the better you do in attracting your significant other.

Unfortunately most couples have neglected the importance of bonding and re-attraction in marriage. They have allowed themselves to be carried away by other commitments which seem relevant at the mean time. All other work you put into building your relationship might prove useless if you lack attraction between each other as couples.

The history of your attraction or attractiveness may not matter when the present state of attraction does not favor your intimacy. How often you have sex have nothing to do with the amount of attraction you have. Sex is an obligatory part of committed relationship and it can easily happen even when no satisfaction can be derived.

Benefits of Having a True Sex with Your Husband

You will achieve satisfaction and content

Achieve good night sleep

Help you de-stress

Regular sex gives your skin a youthful glow

It increases your sex drive

Strengthens your heart muscle

Helps you lose weight

Helps to boost your immunity

Protects your body from involuntary urination

Sex cures headaches

Passion is the function of physical attraction and how this attraction is maintained depends on the strength of your marriage intimacy. Seducing your husband is a very important part of maintaining a physical attraction. Here are some of the consequences of lack of physical attraction in marriages:

Poor sex life

According to a research at the New York State University, couples lacking a significant physical attraction tend to enjoy little to no sex. Their lack of sex can also be related to the amount of stress and burden they feel in the relationship. Significant numbers of such partners often sleep in separate beds and they often accuse each other of never initiating sex. On the other hand, the study result shows that couples may have more sex all the time or be filled with the desire to have sex but the lack of attraction or legitimate sexual intimacy may render the act unsatisfying.

Lack of affection

The lesser the physical attraction the less couples feel real affection towards each other. They might tolerate each other also on the basis of obligation but the affectionate gestures often shown even in their private lives might be little to none. The sexual compatibility that once was felt might remain absent.

There could be less holding hands, less cuddles, less play and fewer ideas for fun or date nights. Affection is also determined by feelings and the extent of this passion by time spent in actualizing the individual action of both couples.

Lack of respect

Attraction brings about respect. Being attracted to someone also means the thought of them keeps replaying on your mind, feeling like most of your activities, your moods and emotional drives are affected by the presence or absence of that person. Without good sex, the conscious value felt between partners will be reduced and lack of appreciation and concern may kick in.

Partners may begin to compare each other with the neighbors, other family members, or coworkers. When you are unhappy with your relationship, it will be easier to disgrace your partner in public or talk about your secret business outside.

Distance

Lack of attraction is first felt when there is an emotional distance. This will lead to mental, and then physical distance. When distance is felt emotionally, it will begin to manifest physically.

Nitpicking

Lack of attracting make partners to stop tolerating their less flattering sides; the simple weaknesses that were once tolerable may become irritating and unwitting. Even the side of your partner that made you admire them for who they are becomes less admirable.

You will begin to criticize your partner on little mistakes or even find a way to make sure they make mistakes so that you can criticize them. These entire acts can be unconscious and partners may not even realize they are doing it for each other until it reaches the worse peak. It is difficult to stop unless realized. Attraction issues based on underlying reasons must be dealt with.

Affairs

The distance, the lack of tolerance and the nitpicking opens a huge loophole for a third-party to interfere with the relationship. Deprivation due to lack of attraction is one of the triggers of marital affairs. When the other person feels neglected, he or she tends to find love in another world, and any opportunity may seem a haven for the unsatisfied body and soul.

The electrifying feeling of feeling attractive and being attracted to someone is all it takes for an affair to be initiated. It begins with mental affair;

fantasizing about being with someone else even during your intimate moments; and then when care is not taken, the physical affair, which is very hard to stop. The worse form of affair is when emotional feelings become the driving force.

Is being physically attracted to your spouse really necessary?

Physical attraction is as important as mental attraction. Both should be maintained for the love to thrive and to be able to feel attracted to each other even at an older age. The longer the relationship, the more mental attraction begins to play a significant role on the intensity of intimacy, and then physical attraction. One cannot do without the other.

Other Books by the Same Author

Before we proceed I'd like to say thank you for downloading this book. I believe the suggestions provided in this book will improve your marriage intimacy to the best. Please, below are other books about marriage and intimate relationship that will also help you greatly in achieving happiness and satisfaction.

1. <u>100 Ways to Cultivate Intimacy in Your Marriage</u>: How to Improve Communication, Build Trust and Rekindle Love

2. <u>232 Questions for Couples:</u> Romantic Relationship Conversation Starters for Connecting, Building Trust, and Emotional Intimacy

The First Stages of Seducing Your Husband

The aim is to keep affection alive in the relationship, to make sure you desire the company of each other in all circumstances.

1. Plan a guy date

First take note of his interests, hobbies and likes. Things that guys like include adventure races, genealogy, drawing and painting, paintball, card playing, learning a foreign language, magic flying, cooking, mountaineering, pool, photography, hiking, marshal art, archery, bowling, model building, fishing, hunting, playing guitar, chess, gardening and sports.

These are exhaustive list of the things a modern man would like to do for fun.

At the first stage of seducing your husband, the aim is to shake off all pressure and make sure you include fun in your relationship. It is an act that brings about emotional stimulation; when your spouse is excited, attraction becomes easy.

Take a simple habit or interest among the listed and plan a surprise date around it. The romantic date in the classy restaurant works, but in this case our aim is to ignite an intense excitement for our seduction plan to work.

For example, if your husband is good at bowling you can plan a date and allow him to teach you. You can also do this with fishing, adventure races, model building and photography. Also your conversation could be about music, politics or sports, whichever one your husband has good interest.

2. Erotic control

A typical woman wants to be dominated in bed, to let her man take charge and do all sorts of things that will make her feel wanted. We all agree with this fact but the 21st century men also like to feel the other side of the fantasy, and many women are able to take advantage of this to create the kind of passion they want during their intimate sessions.

The beauty of taking charge of erotic control is you don't have to try the same thing, the same pattern that has been used in the past. You are free to bring your fantasy into reality, you are free to go wild and make sure that you are satisfied while revealing your wild side to your significant other.

3. The touch

During the actual process or foreplay you should gather the courage to take pleasure in touching yourself and let your husband watch. It doesn't have to be awkward but you can use your hands to do all the magic. Confident women have used this method to seduce their husbands by first touching themselves, and then guiding the hands of their men to the right places—the places they want to be touched.

The emotional sentiment derived through this act is very powerful. If you are afraid that you are going to look awkward during this process, practice it alone in front of the mirror; you will also learn new seductive gestures that showcase your best features as a women.

4. The biting

Although this might look extreme for a conservative husband, biting provides a greater stimulation during intimate sessions. It makes your husband be in the present. In marriage, when the sex becomes boring, a couple will be having sex and still be thinking about work or friends. Biting is one of the acts that will place his minds in the moment.

By playfully biting his neck you are consciously showing him that you are a giver. Using your teeth lightly on his lips while making out shows how badly you want him at that moment. One of the alternatives if you don't think biting is appropriate for your husband; you can try dragging your teeth over his chest or shoulders. Also, be careful not to bite hard so that you don't kill the mood.

5. The tease

When you are having sex with the same person for a long period of time, getting off becomes very important during your sessions. The advantage is you know this person and exactly when they are going to climax. The most seductive wives know that at this stage the man is more vulnerable and they can sure achieve the control they want.

The aim is to keep him at that edge for long so that you will make the necessary tricks that will make you dominate the session; you are practically increasing the value and the need for that particular end point. In whichever act, slow down or even stop moving to allow him move his hips toward you. Your hand or body gestures should take control of the situation for some seconds or a minute before you allow him to explode.

6. Tie him up

This marks the beginning of your dominance. Many women confessed about feeling different the first time they tie their husbands during foreplay. In this case you don't need to buy ropes or extra materials to make your sessions perfect.

The use of bandana or old ties, or even his current ties will do the magic.

The most important aspect of this practice is how you communicate; what you are about to do; how you want it; and the unfamiliar places you will have access to, now that you are dominating your man. Tie his hands above his head or behind his back; whichever works for you, just make sure you take your time and enjoy the moment.

7. Get naked

It is time to take back all the powers you have lost by bringing back the power that Mother Nature bestowed upon you. Getting naked is the first and your most effortless form of attaining power over your husband's mind and actions. You take charge of his thinking, and at the same time take over the moment, sending a direct message that it's time for pleasure.

You can initiate this when just got out of the shower or by wearing a robe with nothing underneath to wait for him as he comes back from work. Most men will be glad to be welcomed with such gift. Also, you don't need to buy sexy lingerie, just allow nature to take place.

8. The dictator talk

There are several patterns of dictator talks that suggest, provide conditions or command a partner to perform an act during intimate sessions. For example;

"Eat my____ right now"

"You know I like it when you____"

"Get your big____ in my tight____ right now."

"You know I love it when you____"

"Take me now"

These are improvised dirty talks that get your bloods running toward a particular end. It can be used to kick start a session or to cause more arousal during the session.

9. Hair-pulling

Hair pulling should occur as an excuse to hold yourself in balance or to let him know that what he just did was just right. Besides, men also like their hair to be pulled or touched when getting intimate. Also, it provides for roughness which is very important for excitement, making the moment desirable, something to look forward to everyday.

10. Spank him

Use your hands to smack him a little, and you can increase the firmness once you realize he is okay with it. This action has become one of the important sex initiating tools for the modern wives. It makes the husband open with the friendliness and kinkiness of the moment that will lead straight to bed.

Most of the times when a woman initiate spanking, the man will often pick it up and use it more often to convey a gesture of desire spontaneously. Married couples should be able to enjoy the arousal that comes with this action without bringing restriction.

11. Undress him quickly

The speed at which you undress your husband may determine the intensity of the desire you have for him, in return he will feel wanted and be stimulated. In fact, the modern woman will just leave the pants around his ankles as she takes him. You can take his clothes off fast or tell him to take them off fast as you are coming to devour him.

This method can be applied when you are trying to take charge of the moment. It allows you to have it your way without limitation and have the kind of session you desire either fast or slow.

12. Undress him slowly

Allow him to listen to the sound of the zipper and the pop sound as you unbutton his jeans. Let the arousal build up slowly as you take your time in bringing him to the Promised Land. This will ensure that you have plenty of time to explore fantasies and now that you are the lead, it may even be more exciting. In this process, do not allow your husband to undress himself, take charge by telling him to allow you undress him.

13. Get grabby

Grabbing a guy's "behind" provides a reassurance and guidance on the way you want to be handled. It encourages your man to realize that he can't be bad for you; it shows lust and the symbol of lost. It shows love and the initiation of intimacy.

You are free to grab him as hard as you want. In fact the harder the better and the more will you encourage roughness and uncontrolled desire towards achieving the goal. During this session you can ask him to grab you as a command. Follow his guide as he gets comfortable grabbing you from behind, he will start to change the position of his hands, you can also do the same thing.

Creating the Atmosphere for Strong Sexual Relationship

14. The communication tablet

Communication is referred according to a study as a key factor in achieving mutual satisfaction. The act of sex alone cannot bring the satisfaction needed in both couples. There must be true intimacy, an emotional connection to be felt and maintained, and for the couples to consciously realize how far the relationship is going.

This starts from practically telling your partner how you feel about sex or the initiation of the act. Talk about what arouses you, what gets you off, what makes you uncomfortable, what turns you off and your best positions. During this communication exercise you need to be able to listen and understand exactly what your husband is trying to say about your sex life.

Make sure that you communicate your needs and also make an effort to understand the need of your man when it's communicated. This way mutual satisfaction will be achieved and during your intercourse you will have more ideas on the things you should do to make it more exciting and spontaneous.

15. The 15 second kisses

Instead of kissing once in a while for a second or two, take your time to kiss for 15 seconds everyday even when it doesn't mean it will lead to sex. The initiation of the 15 second kiss strategy should be discussed between partners and the aim should be uniform.

The important of the 15 second kiss is to achieve a deeper intimacy, to kiss for the love and to feel affection towards each other by actually forcing the affection by the only physical action that will make that possible.

The kissing often leads to love making; you become more intimate with your husband as you exchange deeper emotions all through. Romantic bond is created and partners become more vulnerable. You become weak for each other, only to explore your strengths in the most intimate way possible.

16. Update the lingerie wardrobe

Lingerie is not just important in making you look sexy and more appealing to your partner; it also makes you feel more comfortable and sexy. With the acknowledgment that you will get your husband aroused, you will have a new confidence to reach and do things that will spice up your love life to the best.

The secret lies between the ability to try new styles and how bad you want your husband; depending on how confident and sensual you feel. It is about improving your sex life while making yourself feel good at the same time.

17. Schedule sex

Most experts label scheduled sex as vibe-killer but married couples can have the best sexual satisfaction when they can get it when their body needs it. Most couples tend to forget about sex when they become busy with work and kids. Sex is not a satisfaction to be rendered or achieved only when arousal is presented; it is a primary need of your relationship, a need for your body to stay stress-free and balanced.

The aim for planning your sex is to make sure you look forward to it and to make plans to spice up the activity a little. It provides consistency, which provides reassurance for happiness and long-term fulfilling relationship. So, you should maintain a date for making love, either once or twice per week.

18. Accept the changes

First, you need to accept that how you feel about sex and the act itself changes with time. Secondly, you need to realize that it is your responsibility to adapt with the change, to make sure that you are not left behind with the thoughts of how your sex life could've been.

You need to accept the irregularity but make sure that every time you have the opportunity you make it a significant part of your growth in the relationship. Another way to make sure the intimacy of sex or lack of it does not affect your relationship negatively is to embrace closeness and the pleasure you drive from doing other things together. This way you can also work together in achieving a deeper pleasure during sex.

19. Start with foreplay

Most couples make the mistake of making sex be all about intercourse. In fact the most important part that brings about the needed pleasure is the foreplay. The act stimulates desire and teases the body to wait before getting the satisfaction.

Let the excitement shoots to the peak and make sure the mood is being set in the process. Dirty talks or explorations should be included during this process. Another form of foreplay suggests a non-physical activity which includes sexy texts or notes where your partner will see and get the message.

In this case your mode of description determines the kind of play you are driving your spouse into and for how long it will take before the initiation of physical activity.

20. The bedtime routine

This is referred as the things you do before you go to bed apart from sex or spending time on the internet. One of the most important bed time routine is agreeing to keep your phone away before you go to bed. This provides time for pillow talk or just having an alone time with your husband, which is important in building a greater intimacy.

The aim is to achieve a deeper connection and to involve in passive activities that include sharing a calm time with each other before going to bed.

21. Get ready for new tryouts

Learn something on your own and implement it during your intimate sessions. Do something different from the way you've been doing for years. Reverse that comfortable position and try the things you've been having doubts about. It is the new thing that you can do together that will get your passion and affection for each other alive and confirmed.

Experiment on everything on the bed, outside the bedroom and even in your social life. Experimentation is like an act or exercise that keeps your sexual relationship fit and healthy. It also gives you the chance to feel more comfortable when introducing new things without having doubts about his reaction.

22. Do not neglect the spontaneity

Even though you have scheduled dates for sex and no-sex, it would be great if you are open with unplanned sex. Do not make plan for it, and doing it does not change the dates for the planned. In this case you don't need the bedroom to perform this activity; try the bathroom, living room, basement, or even the car.

You can even bring back the sex routine during the early stage of your relationship and strive to feel the excitement of youthful love once again. Let the pleasure take control, let your body decide for you.

Getting Him in the Mood for Sex (Make Him Last Longer)

23. Body language

The art of seduction demands that your body language should be suggestive to the particular act you want to lure your partner into—and the more sensual the better. For example, a simple hug when done sensually can turn your partner on. Long hugs are very important part of getting your partner in the mood for a long sex.

A kiss on the cheek or neck is also suggestive in bringing about arousal on the side of a man. The longer the kiss the better; and more confident women use the tongue to directly suggest to their partners that they are in the mood for something bigger than a kiss.

24. The dirty talk

This is an opportunity to once again flirt with your husband. Dirty talk works when you whisper flirty words into your husband's ear using the sexiest voice possible. The simple way to start is by complimenting him about his last bedroom performance; get descriptive on how he makes you feel and how you want him to do it again this time.

Compliment your husband about his body part that only you the wife know the advantage. The key factor is flattery; it can get you places you can't imagine and when you focus on the true features and abilities of your husband, you will create the chance for him to even try harder in becoming better at using those features to satisfy you.

25. The eye to eye seduction

Look straight into his eyes and tell him you want him. The kind of look that ignites desire must be deep; it must reassure the meaning of what is coming out of your mouth with the confirmation of lust and depravity. Your voice should also create the tension, to create both play and intimacy; to suggest even when you don't have to use direct words to describe what you want.

For example, "I want to play" or "I want to have fun" are the suggestive phrases you should begin with to provide the particular suggestion. The key to every successful seduction is to begin slowly and light, and then graduate to direct keywords and phrases to provide for instantaneous satisfaction of desire.

This becomes more interesting when your husband knows a little bit about your fantasies. The words you use while looking into his eyes will provide the specific play you want at the moment.

26. Sexting

From time to time, you should text your husband letting him know that you can't wait to get together and have an exciting moment. Use sexy descriptive words like "I'm going to show you crazy love tonight" or "I've got a sexy surprise for you." This is very important to make sure that he is in the mood when you get back home.

Make your spouse wait for you desperately and even give him the hint that you are thinking about him sexually even when you are apart. Passion breeds passion, this act will also bring your husband out of the closet, to make him try something out of the normal way, to make your sex life spontaneous.

27. Hot shower

Take a short shower with your husband to easily set the mood. Bubble bath is the alternative for hot shower in which you could include massage to provide for sensual touch. Let the passion take control of the moment; make sure that you spend a considerable amount of time on foreplay after a long hot shower with your husband.

Fun Ways to Seduce Your Husband

28. Play the new person

This suggests that you create an illusion of variety to spice the entire session. Wear the Halloween costume and play the sexy character with your husband. Resort to any outfit that makes you feel or look like a new person starting from "tight-high boots to a blonde bobbed wig". Let role-playing be simple as possible and the weekends be reserved for a more complicated or sensual role-play.

Let the pretty woman in you come to life. You can also wear the kind of outfits you used to wear while you were still dating in order to bring back the old memory, together with the burning desire you have for each other. Let the moment of first-impressions come to life once again as you take your sex life to the next level.

29. Start the picture trick

Take a picture of yourself from a provocative angle, send one to your partner once in a while or just slip it in his briefcase. More revealing pictures while you leave all another parts to the imagination can also be sent. Let your face be hidden on picture to protect your identity from your spouse. Let him feel connected to your body without the need to know who his on the picture.

The aim is to ignite the desire and want for your body. Let your husband be the one you trust before you perform this act, do not send your provocative pictures to the man you don't trust or when your marriage is "on the rocks". Let there be a passion to be shared, and the act should only be to ignite affection and the desire to have a good time with your significant other. You may wear a new sexy lingerie, the one your husband haven't seen yet, then you can welcome him wearing it when he comes back.

30. The lust notes

The handwritten lust notes are the oldest and most effective ways of describing what you want to do with your husband. They contain details that could only be read by your husband, something graphic and suggestive, something arousing and definitely sexy. The modern wives have now upgraded to using email or text to get this lust messages across.

Send these notes when your husband is in the middle of an important meeting with clients or partners. Write a note and place it on the bed while you are in the shower. When you are in a restaurant, movie theatre or a party you can whisper such details in his ear.

You should use different phrases to describe the same thing in order to keep it new and arousing. You can keep a list of up to ten phrases for particular suggestive moments.

31. The loose hair trick

One of the simple things men find sexy in every woman is a loose hair. Take the time to play with your hair when you are at home and let your husband notice. Take the time to loose your hair and allow him to watch you do it.

32. Wear backless outfit

Backless outfit is very suggestive in terms of both mutual and sexual comfort. Wearing this comfortable cloth at home is a surefire way to attract your husband without going out of your way. When you are alone with your husband, wear something that shows the hint of your waist down to your underwear.

Even better, allow your husband to wonder if you are wearing something under the dress or not. You can include the hair play or remote play in this case. Allowing him to touch you and getting away, to make him chase you. Bringing back the fun will help you achieve a reasonably fulfilling foreplay.

Subtle Ways to Seduce Your Husband and Make Him Desire You

33. Try new clothes in front of your husband

On the basis of wanting to hear his opinion, change into a new cloth in front of him and make sure you strip out of the old one slowly. Allow him to watch as you make sexy gestures and postures.

Going to the store together and taking him with you to the changing room will also ignite the sense of passion and desire; to see you almost naked in a new place is very important for the arousal needed at the moment.

34. Talk about him

This idea might seem random but talking to your spouse about his personality while watching TV or playing card game together builds a new wave of intimacy. Mutual bonding, which is very important in the act of love making, can be easily created. You can also drift to what you want in the sex department and his features that make your wants possible.

The talk should be aimed at making him desire you instead of creating different demands that might overwhelm his nerves. Take a step at a time and go deeper with the sex talk, all being focused on his personality.

35. The massage seduction

Welcome him with an oil massage, romantic music and low lights. Use aromatic candles to set the mood. First you can take him to the shower before the massage so that you can take your time doing it. Ask him to do the same thing and allow it to transcend into a steamy activity.

Let your aim be to help him relieve the stress when he gets back from work, and you should take your time performing the act to make that possible. In order to make the session more sensual you can watch videos on sensual massages and employ some of the methods to get your husband in the mood.

36. Show interest on the right zones

When he comes back from work and he is telling you about his day, show an excessive interest not just on his words but in his body language. Realize when your husband is stressed, totally stressed or extremely stressed. Also, realize when your husband is excited, totally excited or extremely excited.

Sit next to him in order to assess his feelings. Or instead of listening to him with your eyes looking straight into his, play with his hair and ears and put your interest into caressing and making him feel good at the moment. The hair and ears are the weakest zones of the male body that can stair up sexual desire when caressed.

37. Highlight your features

Make your breasts look more tempting by countering or highlighting them; a V-neck will do the trick in this case; just make sure that it doesn't show too much so that your husband won't notice the particular trick.

First you need to make sure that the shirt contour around the edges, and then highlight between them. This brings out the best out of your curves that will make him desire you.

38. Use the power of the lights

Turn off the lights and only allow lights from indirect sources to light the room. Accompany this relaxing and romantic environment with a soft music in order to get your husband relaxed. Take the chance to include either massage or soft long kisses to provide a direct suggestion about the moment.

You can go naked in the dark and allow your husband to only notice when he begins to run his hands through your curves and caressing every inch of your body. Take the time to feel it and mourn to reassure him of your desire to have him right at that moment.

39. The killer perfume

Sometimes smelling good is not good enough to create the arousal you desire but the smell of seduction. One way to smell good in order set the mood is by using a new and pleasant perfume, letting your husband to notice and smell it during a long hug or cuddle.

You should constantly smell good in order to keep your husband wanting more. You don't have to keep changing perfume to stay new but make sure that your husband unconsciously knows that you are going to smell good and there is no turn off during your intimate moment.

40. The nail polish trick

Use an interesting color combination for your nail polish, colors you are sure your husband will like. The aim is to make sure he notices these small changes. Men are visual beings and tend to appreciate changes that provide for enhancement of looks or the provision of a platform that stimulates their desire.

Take your time on the nail polish and always use interesting colors even when it means changing it every week. Sometimes you may leave your nails clean and natural in order to provide another feel of nature and spontaneity.

41. Dance

Dancing is one of the most sensual workouts that improve your bedroom performance. Starting from how long you will be able to hold on, to having the better muscles to provide for acrobatic movements during your intimate moments. Researches have shown that dancers enjoy better sex and derive more satisfaction when they are actively involved in physical activities before getting intimate.

Get yourself in a dark room and turn up the volume of the stereo and dance your way out of your physical comfort zone. Better yet, play a video and follow simple dance moves that will get you creative and going beyond your limits while moving your body. This will provide for excitement and greater joints lubrication that will help you while dominating your intimate sessions.

42. Tell him funny stories

Tell him funny stories in order to showcase your humor side once in a while. The stories could be about your day at work, the kids or something that just happened with a friend.

Tell him about your day in a seductive voice while you unbutton his flyer slowly. Take your time and practice control by telling him not to move his hands, to allow you take off everything and take charge of the moment.

43. Get alone

Once in a while, take a timeout and be with yourself and you alone. Allow him to look for you in the study while you are reading your favorite novel and sipping your favorite coffee or tea. This act should not be purposefully aimed at letting him chase you but to actually create a time where you will dominate and make your husband notice the value you put on self-care.

People with extreme self-love are irresistible. The more you give yourself love and tender care, the more attractive you become even to your husband, and this includes having a quality time of your own.

44. The snack surprise

Surprise your husband with a small snack; serve him like a queen treating her king with love and respect. Feed him the fancy snack and allow him to also feed you. Simple snacks like strawberry sandwich or Nutella can do the magic. The most important aspect of this is how you present it.

The aim is to be romantic and showing gestures that will provide for the hint that your husband is being taken care of in the best way possible. The simple love gestures can bring back the fun in your marriage relationship.

45. Let him watch you do the chores

Perform the simplest house chores such as tidying the couch, folding some clothes or doing the laundry. Take your time and do these chores slowly as he watches you. If you are alone with your husband you can wear a short that will provide the outline of your "behind" as you bend over, also wear a lose top that will provide a substantial amount of cleavage.

Some women have succeeded in seducing their husbands by wearing a short dress while doing simple house chores by allowing him to get a glimpse under the dress by bending over innocently.

44. The seductive eating

According to a study carried out in the University of Amsterdam, men find eating seductive as much as slow dance. This is more significant when they are watching the woman they already knew seductively and slowly eating a snack and sipping a soft drink.

Just the way eating fast is a turnoff especially when you are in the public, eating slowly creates a sexual tension especially when you maintain a significant amount of eye contact during the process. You don't have to eat slowly all the time to remain desirable but applying this technique once in a while will bring about desire and passion.

45. Show too much skin

Do not completely dress up at home; wear something that shows more skin, something that leaves less to the imagination. For example, cotton shirt, shear top, short pajamas or just large T-shirt that goes halfway across your thighs.

The aim is to let your husband acknowledge the fact that a sexy lady is walking around the house; let his focus be aligned to exploring a passionate moment together. You may resort to showing too much skin only the weekends or a day or two around the weekdays.

Things Men Want Women to Do In Bed

46. Ask for more

Most women tend to be quiet in bed and settle for whatever the husband is willing to offer during the bedroom session. The most successful relationship is characterized by the communication of wants and needs, not just one-sided but among both partners.

Men like it when a woman has the courage to ask them for more in their sex life, to demand more time before climax or to make the foreplay last longer; or even to ask your man to be prepared for two rounds today instead of the normal one round per session.

Be a woman that knows exactly how she wants to be treated not just outside the bedroom but between the bedcovers. Make personal plans about how you want the session to progress. You don't have to take the lead to make it happen, communicate what you want and allow him to do exactly what you want. Ask for more from your husband; ask for passion, affection and satisfaction.

47. The look

According to a survey to actualize on the things women are missing that might actually spice up their married life, most men confessed about the need for their women to look at them during sexual activities. Apart from kissing, most men perform better when you watch them do what they love to do with you.

Do not close your eyes in anticipation of ecstasy, let the moment be your ecstasy, lets you derive pleasure in the process not just the end point.

Look him in the eye or watch his movement and even use your hands to control some parts.

48. Let him discover you

Most women tend to be "closed" even with their husbands; they tend to have limitations when allowing their men to explore some parts of their body, so they remain closed down and unsatisfied. The same study shows that men always like to explore the woman body.

Just like any science project, men tend to have the enthusiasm of exploring the body to discover the most sensitive points and to make sure they have the knowledge of every inch of curve. Instead of rushing the process or making it hard for your man to explore, relax and be open. Just lay your body down and let him work his hands around you.

49. Get on top

Although you enjoy sex the most when the man is on top, men also tend to like the idea of you being on top as they watch your body do all the tricks you know in the book.

Being on top also means exploring more sex positions with your husband. Not just about position, whatever you feel like doing in the moment, take part in making sure that it happens, even when it means going rough or including toys.

50. Resort for a quickie

Men are the masters of quick sex, although it doesn't have to be regularly. Use the public bathroom, the car, your backyard or even the garage for a quickie. Take a rush moment and initiate this act, and make sure you get off as fast as your husband. Let that be your little secret and to even intentionally try it when you are bored with the slow bedroom session.

Most couples confessed of public sex when asked about the most exciting and memorable things they have done together. The risk provides a great deal of excitement and you will realize that both of you are aiming towards the same safe haven.

51. Sex in the morning

Most men, if not all, would love to use the morning wood for something really important, something that has to do with pleasure. The morning sex can be quick depending on how much time you have to start the day, but make sure you initiate this by either waking him up with some tickle as you touch the most sensitive part, or you can just surprise your husband by sliding it directly; let him wakeup with the ecstatic feeling. Apparently, morning woods stay longer, so be ready to enjoy the moment as well.

52. They want role-play as much as women want it

Men like to see their women striptease as a form of foreplay. They like to watch you perform all the seductive acts; as you showcase your feminine features that made him fall in love in the first place. The role-play might not turn you on in particular but you can always sacrifice when you realize it turns your husband on.

In this case you should only avoid acts that make you uncomfortable or the ones that can hurt you. You can ask your husband what he wants in this moment in order to do the actual things that will turn him on.

53. Upgrade your spontaneity

A man likes a woman who can have sex in-between schedules, a women that does not make lame excuses when her man is trying to touch her, a woman who is considerate about the deprivation her man is going through when she is busy and make time even when she is busy, just to get together with her husband; a woman that is conscious about the canal needs of her man and make an effort to meet those needs.

54. Become a giver

Men also appreciate a giver of love, a woman who can make love to a man instead of always the other way round. This woman is appreciated among all men and her man knows that he has found a rare woman, the one to spend a lifetime with, having an undying passion and affection toward each other.

She recognized and realized the concept of receiving and giving. She knows when to say "give it to me" and she knows when to say "let me give it to you." Her pleasure is to derive pleasure in pleasuring her man, making sure the satisfaction is constant.

55. Get responsive

Most women tend to lay dead on their backs during sex. Regardless how your man likes sex, it gets really boring when his subconscious does not recognize a love making between two active partners; it would be like a man humping a piece wood/log and getting frustrated in the long run.

Get active with your bedroom activity. You don't have to do anything out of the way; just respond to what you are getting even when it means mourning. The most turn-on is when you respond verbally and with your body. Allow him to feel the confidence in order to continue doing the things that make you feel good.

56. Take your time

Take your time to initiate or follow through when your husband initiated the act. Do not just 'give in' to 'get over with.' Give your attention to the moment; take your time to enjoy every stage of your love making in order to reach real satisfaction.

For your man, it is very important for him to know that you are into the act as much as he needs to be. Your actions and the way you respond in the process are very important in defining whether you are really interested or not. Do not allow him to finish quickly either.

57. The dominance

Once again even the toughest of men have once confessed of the need to be dominated in bed. A dominatrix is very important to men, especially when they spend most of their day controlling people in the place of work or in the house. It makes a man feel like a huge responsibility is being lifted.

It also allows for the man to feel the other side of the bed; how it feels to not be in charge. Most men like a girl that will take over once in a while, a girl with ideas of the most intimate things you can do together.

58. Allow for experiment

Yes, men also like experimentation; whether in terms of sex positions, locations or the entire foreplay pattern. A normal guy loves to experiment only when his partner is down with it, so it would be a total turn-on for your man to realize that you also like experimenting on new things.

No man wants to make love the same way from the beginning of the month to the end, every man needs new ways to do things in order to keep the passion alive.

59. Be yourself and all that you are

From your daily life to your sex life, strive as much as possible to work on your best features as a woman. Realize your physical and mental uniqueness and work with them toward building the irresistible and always desirable personality. Focus on you and you alone and do not allow yourself to be carried away by what is going on in other people's lives.

Do not compare your relationship or husband with a friend. When you discover an idea, try it with your spouse to see if it will work for you. Do not force a new idea. Dispose even the finest idea if you realize it won't work for you; focus on building your own path of love through the discovery of new fantasies. Work on the fantasies you have and the one your husband is dying to try

Make time once in a month to try something you've been afraid of trying and watch yourself grow to become the most significant and attractive person in your husband's life. The real you is dying to come out, to shine and be desired just like any other person; with this you will not only become an object of desire to your husband, but a role-model to other women.

60. Be open minded

Be flexible in allowing for new experiences. Allow your mind to be excited by new adventures that involve sexual and nonsexual activities. Do not suppress your need to try the risky act just because you now see yourself as a mom.

Do not be the one to give excuses about not going on a trip that might involve the best experience of your life time. Stop telling yourself that this is not the right time, for there is never a right time, only you can make the time right.

61. Touch him everywhere

Just the way men love to touch every part of the woman body, they also like to be touched or rubbed. The sensual feeling is not just between men's legs, neck or lips, other parts of the body that needs to be touched include the back, buttocks, chest, chest hair and thighs.

Running your hands on his rough body should be included as part of your seduction to get him in the mood. During sex, touch him in places your hands will reach in order to show that you care about making love and sharing the intimate moment.

62. Masturbate and let him watch

Masturbation in general should be avoided especially when you are doing it to avoid having sex with your spouse or because they can't satisfy you. But during foreplay, masturbation is encouraged to provide for newness in the arousal pattern. Men like to watch as much as girls like to watch.

You can take turns watching each other or do it simultaneously while facing each other as you get off at the same time. The aim is to provide for lust toward your partner and to have the image of them working themselves stuck on your mind; which will increase the sex drive in the relationship. Alternatively you can touch yourself in order to reach a maximum level of arousal, and then initiate sex,

63. Swallow

Since I like keeping my descriptions classy, let's say that swallowing is one of the things men appreciate. Men tend to watch a lot of videos that give them ideas on their likes and dislikes about sexual intimacy.

Some will have the courage to ask you to do certain stuff while some may not be courageous enough. Even when you don't have to swallow, taking your time to play with it using your lips or thumb will provide the arousal needed for the moment.

64. Get filthy

Bring your inner filthiness into the light by telling him using the language, the things you want him to do or the things you are about to do. The filthier the better especially when you resort to roughness.

Men love to hear women talk about the things they like especially during sex. Get rid of all your shyness or being careful about the words that come out of your mouth. Just be a truck driver for the moment and say things relevant for exploring your desire in the moment.

65. Tell him exactly what to do

This is another form of dominance that entails communication but the main aim is to let your man know exactly what you want them to do that will drive pleasure.

Example of the direct things you can tell them to do include "take me from_____", "put your tongue on my___", "go hard when___", or "touch my___".

The talk in this case is not just about filthiness but to make sure that your wants are being directly met instead of anticipating your man to dictate what you want. In return you can ask your husband what he wants you to do. Sometimes during an intimate moment a new idea may come. Do not hesitate to try anything new, go direct to the point and tell him, you are allowed to be loud or even scream.

Fun Dirty Questions To Text Your Husband

66. *"Do you like it when I go down on you?"*

This question can be randomly sent to your husband when he is having a meeting or when you are just thinking about him when he is away. The best time to send this text is when he is an hour away from you. It provides the hint of the things he should expect when he comes back.

67. *"What colors of underwear do you like the most on me?"*

When he texts back, make an effort to wear sexy underwear and welcome him with it. If you don't have that particular color you may choose any color that looks appealing and showcase your sexiness.

68. *"What's your favorite song to get busy to?"*

This provides an insight into the most favorite motion music that keeps your partner going. You should realize that your partner may not have a specific type of music but the text is suggestive enough keep him in the mood.

69. *"What part of your body do you like most when I touch?"*

If your husband is not busy he may find it very interesting to reply the message. It is an opportunity to take the lead and continue sexting, including dirty talks that will keep him aroused.

70. *"When was the last time you went solo?"*

Yes, ask him about the last time he touched himself. If you are bold enough you can tell him that you are touching yourself thinking about him right now and you can't wait to get hold of him.

71. *"How do you want me to touch you? Describe it?"*

This may require more than a text but your husband may take the time to describe how he wants to be touched. Ask him about the last time you touched him, how he felt and whether he wants to be touched the same way today.

72. *"Do you ever have dreams about me?"*

Although this might seem less sexual, the follow up question should be erotic and more descriptive. Take this to the next level by asking the next question.

73. *"Do you like it when I'm on top?"*

At this time you are taking your husband by surprise, leading the way to dirty sexting. This could be initiated even when you are busy at work and you are about to leave and meet your husband at home.

74. *"Do you like being loud?"*

Some men like being loud while some like to keep their mouth shut during sex. If your man replies with yes, tell him how you want him to be loud for you today.

75. *"Do you like playing rough?"*

If yes, tell him that you'd like to play rough tonight. Most men like playing rough and once you set the mood you should be expecting something spontaneous.

76. *"What's your favorite thing to do with me?"*

Every man has a favorite thing to do with his lady, starting from a nonsexual activity to the sexual activity. Ask him to describe how he wants to do this thing to you and how he wants to make you feel.

77. *"How fast can you get here?"*

Now it is time to apply pressure, let your man know that you can't wait to have him; you can't wait to have him take you to the land of fantasy, to reach a point of happiness and to lead you towards a satisfaction.

78. *"Do you want to know what I'm wearing?"*

If your husband is rushing to come home you can tell him that you are not wearing anything or if he has a favorite color of lingerie that turns him on, tell him that you are wearing those at the time.

Sex Questions to Know What Your Husband Likes in Bed

79. *"Is there anything you are afraid of doing in the bedroom?"*

Don't be surprised that your man has insecurity in the bedroom or something he wants to try but is extremely afraid. Asking this question will bring about understanding on the things you could do to provide for better bedroom experience.

80. *"Have you ever been attracted to someone of the same sex?"*

This is the most awkward question that could be asked in the bedroom. If your husband says no you can ask him how he feels about women being attracted to other women.

81. *"What do you think about dirty talk over the phone or Facetime?"*

Know if your husband gets surprised or even feels uncomfortable when initiating dirty talk over the phone. Talk about feelings and emotions surrounding dirty talk and how they affect your moods even when you are in the public.

82. *"What is the best bedroom experience you've ever had?"*

What is the most memorable sexual moment you've ever had as a couple? Does your husband's experience provide an insight into one of the most exciting moments of your married life? Would you recreate this moment?

83. *"How often do you like to be intimate?"*

Men also have the right number of times they want to be intimate, when they feel it is too much and when they feel it is too little. Satisfaction can be determined through the realization of these figures.

84. *"Do you like watching me touch myself?"*

You can ask this question seductively while touching yourself or using the most seductive voice possible.

85. *"Have you ever cheated or been cheated on?"*

This question is all about digging into your past relationships!

86. *"Have you ever done it outside?"*

This question is handy if you have the fantasy of carrying out public sex and you don't know how to communicate the idea to your husband.

87. *"Would you do it outside?"*

This should be your follow up question in order to explore a new level of intimacy with your husband. You will realize that you have a lot of uniform fantasies that are yet to be explored.

88. *"Do you like going down on me?"*

Just the way he may like taking his time to undress you, would he go down on you? Is he afraid that he wouldn't perform well or doesn't have a single idea about how to treat you down there?

89. *"What was your first "adult" experience?"*

Our first adult experience has significant effect on the way we view and perceive intimacy as a whole. Maybe the first adult experience was adventurous, dig into the past to provide ideas for greater experiences in the future.

90. *"What's the new thing you'd like to try in bed?"*

Whether sex position or a longer foreplay, ask him about his ideas that may spice up your love life.

91. *"How many rounds do you think you could go?"*

The answer may depend on the felt efficiency or fantasy, or even the need to be satisfied.

92. *"When we wake up in the morning, what is the first thought that comes to your mind when you look at me?"*

In this case you can share thoughts on how you feel about each other waking up every day to see and to feel. This provides for more intimacy, which guarantees better sex life.

93. "Do you ever have naughty dreams or daydreams?"

Allow your partner to narrate those naughty dreams to you and make sure that you share something naughty that you fantasize about, to ignite sensuality in the moment.

94. *"Do you like cuddling?"*

Most men tend to ignore cuddling but right within them, they know they like cuddling after a long hours of work, sometimes a man just needs to cuddle instead of having sex.

95. *"Which body part are you most proud of?"*

We both know what favorite part a man is always proud of, but asking this question comes with the provision of description that might lead to a stronger sexual intimacy.

96. *"When you are in charge, what is your favorite position?"*

Men noticeably have more than one favorite position. Allow your man to narrate why a position becomes his favorite.

97. *"How did you find out about what you like in bed?"*

Maybe it's an incident, a particular intense moment, or it is about a book he read about sexual satisfaction; maybe it's you that made him discover the best things he loves to do in bed.

98. *"Do you fantasize about me?"*

Ask him where, on what basis and whether something physical made him remember you even when he is working.

99. *"Do you like it with the lights are off?"*

Most men like it with the lights are on while women like it when the lights are turn off, but the purpose of asking this question is to initiate sexy talk at the moment.

100. *"Has anyone accidently seen you naked?"*

This might be an embarrassing moment or a moment that brought about some sense of excitement. You are free to share the details of your own moment also in order to provide for deeper sensuality.

101. *"How old were you when you had your first kiss?"*

This is also about digging into your past to provide for present fulfillment and satisfaction.

102. *"What do you think of open relationships?"*

Have you ever tried open relationship when you were dating, before we met? How does it feel, did you ever felt comfortable sharing one person with another?

103. *"What attempts did you make to woo me? Which ones worked?"*

Take yourselves back to when you were playing hide and seek, when you were playing hard to get while he was making extra effort to get your attention. Realize the charms you had that attracted him to you.

104. *"Would you consider yourself romantic, totally romantic or extremely romantic?"*

What class does your husband fit into?

105. *"Have you ever gone skinny dipping?"*

Make a plan to try skinny dipping even in the house pool.

106. *"Do you prefer having fun in the morning or at night?"*

Check on the trigger points of your spontaneity, to go beyond the sex date, to do something beyond the rules.

107. *"Do you have a name for your package?"*

Every guy has a secret name for his package.

108. *"Do you like experimenting with different positions?"*

It's time to get the best positions to try in the bedroom next time.

Foreplay Tips That Can Drive Your Man Insane

109. Turn up the stereo

Turn up the stereo and grab your husband for a sweet dance. Nothing has to be perfect, just make some time to dance with your husband around the house. As a couple you suppose to have a favorite CD or mix-tape, put that on and go sexy around the house.

Create the most romantic moment at the comfort of your own house. Sometimes music that reminds you of your youthful groove or the early stage of your marriage can get you totally in the mood for some fantasy chase. The stereo has to be really loud in order to feel the music and to allow it to control your minds at the moment.

110. The gift card surprise

Get a gift card to a fancy store for your husband. Go out together and he can choose whatever he wants you to buy. A trip to victoria's secret should be your first guess in order to experience this turn on in being able to choose something really sexy for you.

You can also get a gift card to a favorite men's store to buy his underwear. In this case you can also choose the underwear you want your husband to wear.

111. Play Footsie once in a while.

112. Make a secret appointment with your husband

Take your husband's date planner and mark a day for sex. Actually write "sex at 8pm" on a day's page to get your husband rushing back home for you. This is the surprise you should be making once in a while in order to increase the chances of having a very passionate sex, and to make sure that you show your husband love.

Doing this when your husband is putting long hours and obviously stressed with work will provide him a needed timeout to enjoy real passion.

113. Wear a trench coat and high heels

Wear a trench coat and high heels for a dinner night, nothing under. In this case you have two options: whether to tell your husband that you have nothing beneath the coat at the table or just wait to get back home and tell him. Both will provide the same effect.

Allow him to wonder about the sexiest and craziest act you have pull off and close the night with a passionate sex. The sex drive of your man will elevate to the roof top. Do these once in a while when your husband least expects.

114. Get a baby sitter

Hire a baby sitter for the kids to spend the night at her place, and surprise your husband with overnight sex in the house. This time you can go wild and do it anywhere in the house. You can work around naked in the house and go for several rounds until morning.

Do this on Fridays or Saturdays in order to enjoy long morning sleep after the night. Let the evening be filled with the exploration of fantasies, not just the regular bedroom sex. In fact try as much as possible to avoid the bedroom for the day in order to make the act more spontaneous.

115. Let the friction occur

When you are in the museum or park, brush your husband's arm with one of your breasts. Do this often on the same outing to let your husband get the hint. Let the act be as sneaky as possible so that you can have fun while other people around remain clueless about your devious acts.

When you reach a corner with less distraction you can initiate a long kiss. This also may bring about the idea of public sex in which anywhere safe will do.

116. Create a sexy walk for your husband

Start a sexy walk that only occurs when you and your husband are alone in the house. This might include high heels. When you come home from work, keep the high heel for some time to make sure that your husband notices the walk.

Stimulate his desire to want to take you straight to the bedroom. The walk should be slowly as you sway your hips side to side, letting him have an eyeful of your moving body, and you can create an instant tension which might lead to a long shower and long sex.

117. The kiss distraction

Distract your man with a kiss when you are doing something that does not suggest sex. For example while you are watching a movie with your husband you can take his hands and start kissing his fingers while keeping your eyes locked on his. The look should linger; a better hint to let your husband pause the movie in order to carry out a more intimate activity.

Do these while lying on his lap or when cuddling to provide a loophole for sex. With this initiation, make sure that the kiss lasts longer than normal in order to create a full arousal before the main activity.

118. Whisper in his ears in the public

Whisper something dirty in your spouse's ears complementing him about his shirt, pants or haircut. You can say something like *"you look sexy in that shirt"* and progress into more filthy language to watch how he responds.

119. Remove an item in his presence

While in the living room with your husband, remove your bra or panties while leaving your dress on. This alone should give a hint to your husband that you are ready. If you are shy doing that you can go to the other room and do it but make sure that he notices that something in your dressing is missing.

120. Use feet on his package

Many men have foot fetish, so rubbing your feet around his package can increase the arousal. This practice should be included in your foreplay or use it to initiate an intimacy. If your husband is really into it he might love to suck on your toes or just kiss your feet.

121. Breathe and kiss on the same spot

When you kiss on his neck, breath loudly on the same spot, let the warmth of your breath hit the same spot. If you are comfortable with licking you can also change the temperature of his skin by performing same act.

122. Surprise him like this

When your husband least expected come out of nowhere and initiate a sexual act. Show him openly that you are in the mood and start kissing your husband deeply instead of the normal lip peck.

Another way of surprising your husband is by touching him when you are watching TV even on the night you don't have a sex date. What makes your action awesome is when it's unexpected.

123. Set an alarm

Set alarm 30minutes before your normal waking time, when your husband asks why, you should just initiate your reason. Actually, men like morning sex as much as women, so take your time to have the best intimate moment before you start the day.

Alternatively, you can set alarm to wake you two up in the middle of the night and then initiate the act. This becomes relevant when you do it towards a weekend on Fridays or Saturdays.

124. Use the timeout for a time-out

During a first timeout before a second half of a football game, grab your husband's collar and lead him to the bedroom. If he asks what is going on tell him that this is your idea for a timeout. This act can change the way your husband thinks of you, even when he think you are no fun or spontaneous when it comes to sex.

125. Visit him in the shower

Once in a while, join your husband in the shower and soap his body and just go out. Take your time during this session and make sure you give attention to the sensual places. Do not initiate any intimate activity, just wait for him to finish and meet you on the bed.

126. Leave a trail

Place a trail that will lead your husband to the bedroom when he comes back from work or from the gym. This may include a paper tag with line of kisses that will lead him to the bedroom so he will expect more than kisses.

127. Pretend to be strangers

Act unexpectedly like strangers on a dinner date, start by introducing yourselves then start flirting. Ask him dirty questions and drift to what you would like for sex and what an ideal love making looks like to you. Playing strangers is very important to get both partners excited, you can even tell the 'stranger' what you wouldn't tell your husband about your fantasies or the things you would like to do on bed tonight.

You should be descriptive as possible in order to provide for excitement. Make sure you make your husband to badly need to get you on bed that night, and when you get to bed, make sure you have the wildest sex you could think of.

128. Drink before the act

Light on candles and pour him a drink. Sip slowly and talk before initiating the act. Drinking on bed clear your heads and make you have the most spontaneous sex, even wild and satisfying.

129. The nap time

While resting on the couch with your husband, tell your husband its nap time and walk slowly towards the bedroom while taking off one piece of clothing and throwing it on your way. Make sure your husband is watching you. Make sure that you are lying naked on the bed as he gets to the bedroom.

Pretend to continue to sleep while your husband kisses and caress your body. If you can hold on for a long time, keep on 'sleeping' and allow him to just satisfy your afternoon and still lay on the bed for some time after the act.

130. Shave his beard

Shaving your husband's beard is one of the most intimate and sensual activity that bring your bodies closer even though you are not really having sex. Take your time to clean his face before proceeding to going up all over each other to relieve the tension.

Shaving your husband could be learned and perfected with practice. It demands a lot of focus but gives you a chance to do something together, something your husband never does with anybody else.

131. Run your fingers through his curls

For men, this is the favorite thing women can do to them in the world. No man can resist the tension being built and the pleasure being felt when a woman runs her fingers through his curls.

132. Tease him and get rough

Combine teasing and getting rough at the same time. Not even foreplay, during the actual act; make sure that you tease your husband while taking control of the situation. Show your husband that you really want to take control and you will be using your feminine charms to do that.

First, you can decide to deprive him from getting what he wants at the time he wants it, kiss him and get him close, then pull away; all these acts keeps the tease alive and make your session more interesting.

133. Surprise your husband with something sexy

Shop for new sexy outfits but don't show them to your husband. Pick out a day and walk in wearing the outfit with a pair of high heels to put your husband in the mood. You don't have to do this all the time but taking your time to do this among other things will create the tension and spontaneity of a happy relationship.

134. Build up a tension

Among sexting, body rubbing or allowing your husband to get a glimpse of what you are wearing underneath, creating tension is another way of achieving a deep sex intimacy.

135. Grind on your husband

While still fully clothed, grind against his thigh to show that you are turned on and can't wait to get in the zone. Dry humping can be included where appropriate in order to build the tension and provide for boost of desire for each other.

136. Massage his feet

This action is aimed at relaxing your husband in order to create a smooth arousal. Stress is an obstacle in achieving great intimacy, and the more relaxed a person is the better he will perform in bed.

Foot massage helps in counteracting the cortisol levels, therefore granting the chance to have an increased mood that connects to sex. The concentration level is increases significantly. This means your husband will be able to concentrate on you fully instead of the pile of work he has to finish in the office.

137. The 90-second make-out

The longer the passionate kiss the most likely it will lead to a passionate sex. Even when kissing doesn't lead directly to sex, it provides excitement especially when fondling and touching is included.

The purpose of long kiss is to build anticipation, to stimulate the sex drive, to keep it alive, wanting more and more all the time. It aids the concentration on intimacy in a long-term relationship, and all the skipped sex-dates will be taken care of.

138. Arm wrestle

Compete with each other on simple things; these include arm wrestling, board game, mountain climbing and running. Competition helps the testosterone level to spike up, which means both of you will be aroused for a longer period of time. Apart from the effect of competition on testosterone level, anything that lead to increased heartbeat lead to increase in affection, therefore increased intimacy in the entire marriage.

You can also go for sport games regardless how bad you are at it, the aim is to sweat together, to have a good time, to get out of your comfort zone for a while and even achieve something more exciting regardless of the value. You can also ask your husband to couch you on one of his favorite games, so that you will learn and motivate each other at the same time.

139. Make the face expression

Studies have shown that unlike the way arousal can be dictated physically in men by women; men can't tell if women are in the mood just by watching their body. Your husband can only tell whether you are in the mood or not; whether you are enjoying yourself or not by the expression on your face.

You can tell by looking at his body whether he is in the mood or not. So, part of your job is making the exact face expression for the purpose of showing that you are in the mood. You need to indicate enjoyment or interest by the way you look at him in order to initiate an intimate session. The first step in achieving that is by staring into your husband's eye.

Ways You Can Immediately Spice Up Your Sex Life

140. The no clothes allowed policy

Put aside a day where you cook or order your favorite food and stay at home all day with your husband. On that day, no clothes are allowed. In fact on that day, you are to turn off all your phones and the internet. The only thing allowed is the food, the TV and the pool.

The purpose is to explore each other and to make sure you focus on your bodies and how you will enjoy the moment without being distracted by other responsibilities. So all schedules must be cleared and even the urgent of all should be shifted to the next day.

141. The pause and start mechanism

Watch a TV Show together and use the commercials for make out. As soon as the show is back, pause your make out and concentrate on the show. Plan your sex or no-sex even after the show and watch your desires for each other elevate.

When you make the rules and follow them with your husband you will realize how easy it is to have fun without going out of your way, spending too much or even going out of the house.

142. Use the pillow

The missionary can always get boring but one way to change the sensation is by putting pillow under your hips. Everything changes, you feel more sensation and your husband also will feel your tightness the more.

In this case you can squeeze your legs tighter while loosening it for some seconds. This will make the session more interesting and you will get off faster without the need for roughness or other external sources of stimulation.

143. Delay

Tease your husband by not getting ready in time. Use the time when he is ready and waiting for you, to keep changing between bra and panties, and make sure they are sexy. Seeing you almost naked trying to get ready is a complete turn on that may lead him to want to have some immediately.

Do not let it happen at the time, but make sure you prepare for a passionate moment after you get back home. The purpose here is to increase anticipation, not mental but emotional, not just emotional but sexual. To make sure your husband is thinking about you or even fantasizing about a good time together while he is still at work.

144. Just do it, even when you don't feel it

Sometimes you may not feel the need to have sex after dealing with responsibilities. Even when all you need is a good night sleep, initiate the act. Command the juices to start flowing and you will be surprised where they will take you.

Do not always wait to see or feel something that will stimulate your desire. You don't have to be in the mood to allow your husband to have some, just go with the flow and allow your body to make the decisions.

145. The morning oral

Once in a while, wake your husband with a steamy oral. It doesn't have to lead to sex. Just give him something to think about while sitting in the meeting or when he is performing some office task.

You can send him a dirty sex as a follow up to create more tension and anticipation of a good time. Send him a text that demands a reply so that you can both get distracted by each other, thus creating a greater stimulation for future exploration.

146. Keep the high heels on

When you are about to start the business, wear your high heels and tell him that you are keeping those on. There is one thing about men obsessing about women in high heels that make bedroom activities really steaming. It is both sexy and classy. It reminds them of the attractive **you** they see outside, the one without clothes except for the high heels.

While high heels are hot, other unsexy shoes can be a turnoff during your bedroom session. So you don't have to keep them on. Another thing you can keep on during a quickie is your dress. You can take off the panties and bra, and just lift the dress up to have a good time. This is another twist that guarantees more passion.

147. Follow the 3 stages slowly

Start from the initial stage of making out. Take your time to make out without the need to proceed to the next stage.

Get to the next stage of foreplay and also take your time exploring each other's sensual corners. You can proceed to the next stage only when you can't take it anymore.

When you finally move into sex, make sure you perform all the tricks to make it last to enjoy the ride, not just the destination. To make sure that all the tension built during the first and second stage are released.

148. The end of the day trick

Your man will always appreciate a hand job at the end of stressful day. Intimacy is not always about sex. Take your time to focus only on relieving his stress and concentrate on other things. So it doesn't have to be everyday but it will remain significant in keeping the sex in your marriage alive.

149. The extra something that will lead to sex

Instead of initiating a sexual act, create an atmosphere that suggests or leads directly to sex. Example, put on lingerie; play romantic music; watch a romantic movie, light candles, dim the lights or spread rose petals on the bed.

Sometimes after a hectic day, both of you need extra something to stimulate your desire of having the bedroom activity. So do whatever comes to mind that can create the moment.

Ways to Attract Your Husband Sexually Without Even Trying

150. The power of positive attitude

Although this is the oldest tip in the book, positive attitude is not a passive way of handling relationship but it is an attribute that provides power over circumstances. A positive attitude gives power to control both negative and positive situations.

Circumstances cannot have power over you. Things may not always workout the way you planned. Instead of blaming yourself and replaying the incident, feeling bad constantly, a single courageous positive attitude can turn all that around.

Regardless of your husband's weakness when it comes to sensitivity, your positive attitude can never remain hidden. The positive disposition and outlook make you even more attractive, so it has a significant effect on the amount of passion you can cultivate in your marriage relationship.

151. Flatter your husband once in a while

Normal compliments work magic but fettering your husband sets a new edge to passion and explorations. The engine parts of your relationship that have not been moving for a while will start to move when you put the work in making your husband feel good about himself.

The aim is to make him feel like the most loved man on earth. In your conversation start by appreciating his little efforts, how he works hard to see that the house is in order.

Also, compliment his personality and you can drift to sex talk. This provides a chance for your husband to be open about things he would like to try or even respond by complimenting you about your best features.

152. Flaunt your body to your husband

Flaunt your body to your husband and focus on the features you are most proud of. Wear clothes that will showcase your curves once in a while. Turning into a mom should not make your outlook dull and unappealing.

Remind him of the girl he fell in love with. Sometimes it is not just about seeing you without clothes; it is about seeing you with clothes and wanting to see you without clothes.

153. Boast the make-up kit

Even on Saturdays, beautify yourself for your husband. Let you have a good time while still wearing your make up. Look your best even when you have to wear less. Do not ignore the lipstick that make your face look younger and the nail color that make you look like the party girl.

Do not forget that men are visual creatures and they are stimulated by what they can see and touch at the moment. Sexual attraction is achieved when the face looks appealing as well as the other parts of the body.

154. Keep the distance

Take a timeout, away from any sexual activity or physical touch. Keep some distance in order to get your husband to miss you, and to also allow his desire for you and your company to increase. You don't have to kiss every day to keep the love alive.

Sometimes what keeps your relationship alive is doing the opposite of calling, texting or even sexting. Allow him to come to you. Allow his desire to drive him to you. Allow him to make an effort to seduce you, to make you feel wanted. This will also increase the spontaneity of your bedroom session.

155. Sleep together

One of the killers of romantic relationship is when couples begin to sleep on separate beds. Greater intimacy is achieved when couples sleep on the same bed and wakeup on the sides of each other. It provides time for small talk before bed and also to feel each other in the morning.

It also provides more chances for having a good time before getting out of the bed. Cuddling will improve and you can easily find affection in your marriage. It is important also for couples to go to bed at the same time.

156. Make your sex sacred

Give more attention to sex, just the way you give good attention to your business. Have an undistracted attention on the activity; make it special for you and your spouse.

157. Choose your best priority

Apart from feeding your husband with sex, one thing that will make him desire you when he feels like he is a great priority in your life. Do not make him a Second in your decisions unless when necessary. Give your husband time, listen to him and make sure you understand his needs, whether emotional or physical.

Understanding your husband is one of the most important gifts that cannot be bought with money. Affection breeds affection: so building a strong relationship, devoid of resentment or dissatisfaction, your sex life will also improve. You will have more effect on your husband sexually when you show affection and he has affection for you.

158. The admiration gem

Show that you admire your man by action. Again admiration provides a platform where your husband will feel loved and cherished. Admire his looks, his work ethics, his effort or even the less flattering sides of his personality. Admire the fact that he is becoming a better spouse for you.

159. Keep the libido alive

Most women ignore the fact that some activities they ignore make the libido inactive, which renders their sex drive inactive as well. For example, lack of exercise and eating unhealthy food has strong effect on your sex drive.

Some of the things you eat can destroy your libido. Take more milk and egg, and involve in actual exercises. Dancing is one of the best exercises that increase the libido.

160. Collaborate with your husband

Collaborate in order to achieve a greater satisfaction in your bedroom activities. Being able to work together towards reaching a particular aim means compromising some of your wants, sacrificing some of the things you feel are important and also do things even when you are not totally comfortable. Welcome new ideas and work as a team into making it a reality, to achieve the pleasure intended.

161. Open mindedness

Be open-minded and flexible. Talk about sex like you will talk about any other important aspect of your life. Work with new details all the time and never fail to notice the changes going on overtime. This will make you less predictable, by which excitement will be easily achieved.

By being open-minded you will never see the end point of the possibilities of intimacy in your marriage. Do not work with the blueprint all the time; focus on providing spontaneity when opportune.

162. Provide the periodic get away or at least welcome it

Some men will come with the idea of a periodic get away from your hectic lives, to spend a weekend in the hotel or out of town. You should welcome this idea and postpone all your plans until you get the fulfillment, while enjoying the adventure.

Do not let your partner go alone when there is a chance you can be together on a particular trip. You can also create this kind of getaways in order to provide for more physical activities. Even a simple picnic, involving a wide open space will do the trick in providing excitement and responsive intimate moments.

163. Change the wardrobe

Take your time to realize what you can improve in your wardrobe and create a change immediately. Changing your wardrobe has effect on how sexier you will look for your husband. The idea is to maintain your attractiveness and to act immediately you feel like your husband is not attracted to you anymore.

Go for the trendy and attractive, something that will suite your weight and body type at the moment. You should also consider your age when choosing clothes. Do not go for something that will make you look older and also, you don't have to wear clothes that will make you look slutty.

164. Make his favorite meal

If you've been married for some time you must have noticed that the way to your man's heart is through his stomach. Good food overcomes all the obstacles in marriage relationship, even for the mean time.

You can also invite him in the kitchen so you can play while cooking his favorite meal. Use spices that will improve the mood and also create aroma even before the food will finish cooking.

165. Be emotionally available

Men can be as emotionally weak as women; you just need to understand the moment when your husband needs your support. Sometimes he will need you to just listen to him, to show that you understand what he is going through and offer the word of encouragement, just to keep his spirit up.

Make sure that your husband knows that he can confidently confide in you when he is going through a certain emotional breakdown. Let him call you even when you are away to discuss something that is bothering him about work.

You can place his head on your lap and run your hands through his curls in the moment. By this you will earn more respect and he will be unquestionably devoted toward you even when everything is fine. The affection in your marriage also increases.

Phrases That Turn Guys On

166. *"So, I had this dream last night..."*

Start with this line and come up with something interesting, something that will get you both in the mood. You can tell him about a short encounter with a stranger in your dreams or about you two performing a risky sexual act.

Let your fantasy come out to light. If your fantasy is bondage, describe how it is done. When it becomes a dream you will feel less shy.

167. *"I want to watch"*

Men are sensitive about this phrase even when it means watching them doing nonsexual activities. Maybe you want to watch him play a softball with his buddies or maybe you want to watch him play with his package in the bedroom, whatever you want to watch just make sure you are direct to the point and the watching will lead to some steamy activity.

168. "SWEAR"

During your bedroom session you are free to swear or talk dirty to your husband. Most men prefer women that talk during sex instead of the quiet ones and the favorite talk is the dirty talk.

This also includes narrating the kind of action you want; where you want his hands to go; or how rough you want it to be. This action keeps partners in the moment and satisfaction is easily achieved.

169. *"Touch me right there"*

Tell him exactly what you want in order to reach the edge of ecstasy. He may just know exactly what gets you in the mood but reminding him during the session is very important in achieving deeper and precise exploration of your sexual potentials. It also helps you discover new ways to provide exciting sensation together. And the most important part, men love hearing it.

170. *"I give you permission to wake me up if you get honey"*

This provides an immediate excitement, an anticipation of something more than just a sex. It also becomes relevant when you are very busy with the kids or work, or when your husband has to work late.

You can reassure your husband that he can give you a hint whenever he feels the need to relieve his tension after the stressful day. Also, you will give him the chance to plan for a better intimate moment.

171. *"All during my meeting today, I was thinking about doing this"*

Take your husband by surprise and reveal the secret thoughts you've been having at work. For some reason, men find this really arousing. And knowing that you were busy with work but still thought about him will make him feel like a real priority in your life, therefore boosting his confidence in trying something that will provide for excitement.

Also, you can actually wonder your mind with sexy thoughts about your husband while working. Think about how his lips feel and how his body was all over you last night.

172. *"Yep, that was perfect"*

Let him know exactly how he rocked your world. You are indirectly telling him to do the same thing again by telling him it was perfect. Even if you are the type that makes a lot of noises, just make sure you use the right phrases that will get your husband going.

173. *"I love the way you smell"*

He doesn't have to wear a perfume for you to love the way he smells. He might be sweating and smelling manly but telling him you love the way he smells will make him feel, well, manly, even if he knows it isn't the most pleasant smell.

Natural scent is intimate; couples recognize each other by smell. It is important to let your man know how his smell turns you on especially when you are suggesting that you should have a good time.

174. *"I want you in my mouth"*

Most men realize that women commit to this act as a sacrifice. In this case you can offer this as a gift to show that you have interest in what he loves. Reassure him that he can let go and focus on his happiness at the moment.

Knowing that your man is happy will also enhance your happiness. The aim is to show enthusiasm in working work on his package, proving that you are confident in taking charge of the situation.

175. *"Status update"*

Tell him what is going on with your body at the moment. Tell him the status of your feeling and the effect of what he just started. Tell him whether something he just started is working or not.

Tell him what is more pleasurable and what is more enticing and fun. Let reassurance become a part of your talk during your intimate moments.

176. *"I like being told what to do"*

Sometimes your husband will just assume that you know what to do, or even feel the need to initiate everything in the sex department. Telling him what to do mean achieving a reasonable level of excitement and satisfaction; the aim is to make sure he is enjoying it as much as you are.

177. *"We fit so well together"*

You can mean this either physically or emotionally; they all work in providing for greater intimacy. You can tell him with a sexy voice before or during your intimate moment. You can also send it as a text randomly, as a form of good communication.

178. "I'm about to come"

This is very common but often ignored by most couples. Yes, you should make the announcement. This phrase provides strong effect on your husband; he may begin to go hard or slower just to tease you.

179. *"Whisper what you are doing to me"*

Also you can whisper what you want him to do to you. The effect of whispering to your bonding as partners is enormous. Even outside the bedroom, utilize the power of whisper to improve your intimacy.

180. *"Anything... just say it in a foreign language"*

You can initiate this by starting with some phrases you know in Spanish or French, even Arabic. This will encourage your husband to also include phrases in foreign languages that describe his excitement at the moment.

181. *"Complement my genitalia"*

Make an unusual demand for a compliment, something that can only be said inside the bedroom. You can also compliment his own for a start, and go deeper describing how it affect you using dirty words. Go direct to the point.

182. *"This is my happy place"*

Let your husband realize that you are in a happy place when you are on top of him. Let him realize that being extremely close to him is the happiest place you would want to be all the time.

Ways to Guarantee You Will Have Sex Tonight

183. Arm wrestle

This is among the physical activities that provides touch, and spike your testosterone level.

184. Look at old pictures together

The aim is to trigger those amazing memories, to remind yourselves of the past, when you can have sex like 3 times a day. Photos from your honeymoon should provide that feeling, the want, to stimulate your effort in providing the same affection, wistfulness and tenderness at this stage of marriage.

185. Drink pomegranate juice together

This substance boosts men's sex drive especially when it involves a visual of scantily clad female on the screen or in the physical. Also according to a study at the Sussex University, Pomegranate Martini makes men last longer, with a stronger sex drive, 16 percent higher than before.

186. Play Footsie

Flirt with your husband while watching TV or having a dinner in a fancy restaurant. Rub your foot along his calf or ankle while looking at him straight in the eye.

187. Hug longer today.

189. Wear a red dress to boost your attractiveness level.

190. Open up a box of chocolates to improve your hormone, inducing the relaxed feeling of pleasure.

191. While still outside, Use the secret signal you have as a couple to give your husband a sign.

192. Snuggle on the couch. Cuddle for some time and allow your body to work you toward the pleasure point.

193. Watch porn together.

194. Get into a deep conversation.

195. Go panty-less and make sure he knows

196. Unexpectedly, tie him up

197. Walk away, and do the hip sway

198. Bite your lower lip to draw his attention

199. Mid-dinner, hand him your panties

200. Remove your bra seductively while he is looking.

201. Tell him to expect a surprise when he makes it back home early today

202. Answer the door partially naked

203. Pull his clothes and attack him with kisses and bites.

BONUS

Things that turn men off

These 5 things are the common things women do unconsciously that turn their men off. Regardless of the effort you put into spicing up your sex life, these attributes can make your effort worthless.

When you don't have real interest outside marriage, kids and work;

When you don't keep friends; male or female friends;

When you bad-mouth other women;

When you don't listen, but like to keep on talking;

When keep bringing up the same problem even when you have talked about resolving them.

Other Books by the Same Author

1. <u>100 Ways to Cultivate Intimacy in Your Marriage</u>: How to Improve Communication, Build Trust and Rekindle Love

2. <u>232 Questions for Couples:</u> Romantic Relationship Conversation Starters for Connecting, Building Trust, and Emotional Intimacy

Made in the USA
Middletown, DE
18 February 2018